Restorative Practices in
Elementary Schools

PERSPECTIVE

By Renee Kenady

Published by Martha Renee Creative Sedro-Woolley, Washington

ISBN: 979-8-9939146-8-8 First Edition, 2026

This book is a work of professional educational guidance. All stories, examples, and scenarios are drawn from real school experiences but are presented in ways that protect the privacy and dignity of students, families, and staff.

"Perspective"

Restorative Practices in Elementary Schools

Created and published by
Martha Renee Creative
A registered DBA of Kenady Enterprises
Visit: KenadyCollections.com

Inspired by my career experiences in
Education, youth services
and life in general.

Special Thanks

To the Bellingham School District, whose leadership in implementing restorative practices and professional development shaped my understanding and continues to inspire this work.

I authored this book to share the lens that shaped my work with children and the adults who care for them.

"Perspective" is built on the real
emotional patterns I witnessed in
elementary schools.

Its purpose is simple: to help adults see children with greater understanding, and to offer restorative practices that honor their growth, dignity, and humanity.

Restorative Practices for Elementary Schools

Foundations & Influences

Restorative Practices don't exist in isolation. They grow out of decades of work in psychology, education, and community building. The ideas in this guide are shaped by several key influences that have helped educators understand human behavior, belonging, and accountability in   deeper ways.

Adlerian Psychology & Rudolf Dreikurs

Alfred Adler believed that all human beings are driven by two core needs: belonging and significance. Rudolf Dreikurs brought these ideas into schools, showing that behavior is communication — a child's way of trying to meet those needs. This insight continues to shape modern approaches to classroom culture and student behavior.

Social-Emotional Learning (SEL)

SEL frameworks highlight the importance of emotional literacy, empathy, and responsible decision-making. Restorative Practices complement SEL by offering real, relational opportunities to practice these skills in daily school life.

Indigenous and Community-Based Traditions

Many restorative practices used in schools today draw inspiration from Indigenous traditions around the world — including First Nations circle processes in Canada, Māori family group conferencing in Aotearoa New Zealand, and Navajo Peacemaking in the American Southwest — all of which emphasize relational accountability, community healing, and restoring balance.

Positive Discipline (Jane Nelsen)

Positive Discipline made Adler's ideas accessible to educators and families. It emphasizes encouragement, shared responsibility, and the belief that children learn best when they feel safe, connected, and capable. The language of "belonging and significance" is a main focus of this work, and it remains a powerful lens for understanding student behavior.

Restorative Practices

Restorative Practices build on these foundations by giving students — and adults — structured ways to strengthen relationships, repair harm, and understand their impact on others. Circles, restorative conversations, and community agreements create environments where belonging and significance are not just ideas, but lived experiences.

Why These Foundations Matter

Together, these influences shape a
simple but powerful truth:

*Children learn and grow when they feel safe, valued,
and connected. And adults do too.*

Restorative Practices bring these ideas to life in classrooms, hallways, staff rooms, and school communities —
helping everyone feel they belong, that they matter, and
that they can repair harm when it happens.

Chapter 1
What Restorative Practices Are (and Aren't)

Restorative Practices aren't a program, a curriculum, or a new set of rules. They're a way of creating a school environment where people feel safe enough to learn, speak honestly, make mistakes and repair harm when it happens. And harm will happen—because we're human, and because children are still learning how to be in the world.

For years, schools have relied on discipline to manage behavior. Sometimes it works in the moment, but it rarely changes anything beneath the behavior. Kids learn to avoid getting caught, not how to understand themselves or others. They learn to shut down, not open up. They learn that mistakes make them "bad," instead of seeing mistakes as part of growth and being human.

Restorative Practices shift that. They help students develop intrinsic accountability—a sense of responsibility that comes from within, not from fear. When kids feel safe—truly safe—they can be honest about what happened, how they feel, and what they need to do to make things right. They learn how to repair harm—not just apologize, but truly repair—and to understand how their actions affected others. That kind of intrinsic change lasts and it is a visible relief to the people involved.

This work gives every child a voice. Not just the outspoken ones. Not just the confident ones. Some children are bright, kind, and full of potential, but still afraid to take those risks that would embarrass them. You know the saying, "Better to remain silent and be thought a fool than to speak and remove all doubt". I was one of those kids. If I had been in an environment where I knew I could make a mistake and still be supported—not laughed at, not dismissed—I would have flown so much higher. Restorative Practices create that kind of environment. They make room for every student to be heard, valued, and encouraged to become the best human they can be.

And this work starts with us. Adults have to experience the same kind of sharing, listening, vulnerability and accountability we ask of students. When staff feel safe with each other, they create classrooms where students feel safe too. And when students feel safe, they take risks, try again, and grow.

Chapter 2
Why Safety Comes First
(Adults and Students)

Safety is the foundation of all Restorative Practices. Not physical safety, per se—though that matters too—but emotional and relational safety. When students feel safe, seen, and know they will be held accountable in consistent, predictable ways, it creates the strong emotional boundaries children need and crave. Unpredictability creates fear, and fear leads to emotional bursts that are far more likely to escalate into physical aggression. Safety is what makes honesty possible. Kids can't tell the truth if they're afraid of being shamed. Adults can't model vulnerability if they're afraid of being judged. Without safety, everything else becomes performative: circles fall flat, conversations stay shallow, and repair becomes something students do to get out of trouble instead of something that changes them.

For administrators, understanding this is essential. Emotional and relational safety aren't just classroom practices—they're leadership practices. When staff feel safe, seen, and held to consistent expectations, predictability creates a stronger teaching community. It strengthens collaboration because honesty becomes possible, and it strengthens pedagogy because teachers build stronger and more honest relationships with their students. Unpredictability creates anxiety, and anxiety fuels emotional reactivity. A school where adults feel safe with each other becomes a school where students feel safe too. Leaders set the tone, and the tone becomes the culture.

Chapter 3

Circles: Building Community and Trust

Morning circles are where students' stories are heard — where they share pieces of their lives, build connection, and experience significance and belonging through routine and community. A morning circle is a simple, predictable routine that starts the day with connection. Students sit in a circle so every face can be seen, and each person has a brief chance to share, listen, or respond to a prompt. It's not about solving problems — it's about building community through shared stories, gentle structure, and the feeling that every voice has a place. Morning circles create the emotional readiness that makes learning more accessible and deeper restorative work possible later.

Restorative circles create an honest way to generate accountability where every voice is heard. They are guided by a structured process of questioning that helps students look at what happened, understand the impact, and participate in repair.

The questions themselves come later in the book, but the purpose is always the same: to create a safe, predictable path toward truth, responsibility, and restoration. In restorative circles, students learn that accountability is not punishment — it's a shared process of understanding what happened and how to move forward together. Morning circles build the community.

Restorative circles protect it.

Chapter 4

Restorative Conversations & Questions

Before we look at the questions themselves, it's important to understand why they matter. Restorative questions give students a predictable path to move from emotion to reflection, and from reflection to repair. They help students slow down, think clearly, and understand the impact of their actions without feeling shamed or attacked. The questions also support the adult by providing a steady structure to follow, especially in moments that can feel tense or emotionally charged. These questions aren't a script — they're a guide. And when used consistently, they create the safety students need to be honest, accountable, and open to repair.

When Harm Has Occurred (Student Who Caused Harm)

Adult Language

What happened?

What were you thinking at the time?

What have you thought about since?

Who has been affected by what you did? In what way?

What do you think you need to do to make things right?

Kid-Friendly Language

What happened?

What was going on for you when it happened?

How are you feeling about it now?

Who do you think was affected or hurt?

How were they affected?

What can you do to help fix it or make it better?

When Harm Has Occurred (Student Who Was Harmed)

Adult Language

What happened?

What did you think when you realized what had

happened?

What impact has this had on you and others?

What has been the hardest part for you?

What do you think needs to happen to make things right?

Kid-Friendly Language

What did you think or feel when it happened?

How has this affected you?

What has been the hardest part?

What would help make things better for you?

13

Restorative conversations are where the questions come to life. They are calm, human moments where an adult helps a student move from what happened to what needs to happen next. These conversations don't require a formal circle or a big audience. Most of the time, they happen quietly — at a desk, in the hallway, or during a natural pause in the day. What matters is the tone: steady, curious, and free of judgment.

When adults use restorative questions consistently, students learn that accountability is not something done to them. It's something they participate in. They learn that telling the truth is safe, that repair is possible, and that relationships can be restored. Over time, restorative conversations become part of the classroom culture — a predictable way of handling conflict that protects dignity and strengthens trust.

And as they become part of the daily rhythm, restorative conversations grow into a shared language across the school community. Students, teachers, and families begin to use the same words, the same questions, and the same approach to repair. This shared language creates coherence — a sense that everyone is working from the same values and moving in the same direction.

Restorative conversations are not about perfection. They are about presence. They remind students that even when harm happens, the community still holds them, and there is always a path forward.

Chapter 5

Repairing Harm: From Simple Conflicts to Class-Wide Issues

Repairing harm is the heart of restorative practice. It is where the questions, the conversations, and the community values come together in real time. When harm happens — whether it's a small conflict between two students or a disruption that affects the whole class — the goal is always the same: to restore safety, dignity, and connection. Repair is not about blame. It's about helping students understand impact, take responsibility, and participate in making things right.

Not every situation requires a full restorative circle. Many moments can be addressed through a brief restorative conversation, a quick check-in, or a simple repair action between two students. Other situations require more structure — a small circle, a facilitated conversation, or a class-wide reset.

What matters is that the response matches the level of harm, not the level of adult frustration.

Restorative repair is not a single strategy. It is a continuum. And when adults understand that continuum, they can respond with clarity instead of guesswork, and with consistency instead of reaction.

Simple Conflict Example

Two students argue over a pencil.

Response: Quick restorative moment.

"What happened?"

"How did that affect each of you?"

"What needs to happen now?"

Restorative Conversation Example

A student rolls their eyes and mutters something hurtful.

Response: Restorative conversation.

"What was going on for you when that happened?"

"How do you think that impacted me?"

"What can you do to repair that?"

Small Circle Example

Three students have been excluding a classmate.

Response: Small restorative circle.

Each student shares impact.

They co-create a plan for repair and inclusion.

Class-Wide Repair Example

A substitute reports that the class was disrespectful and unsafe.

Response: Class-wide circle.

"What happened?"

"How did this affect our class?"

"What do we need to do to move forward?"

⭐ *Re-Entry Circle Example*

A student returns after suspension.

Response: Re-entry circle.

"What support do you need coming back?"

"What do we need to know to help you be successful?"

"How can we move forward together?"

Repairing harm is not about having the perfect response. It's about choosing the level of repair that matches the level of harm and doing so with consistency, calm, and care.

When adults respond this way, students learn that conflict is something they can navigate, not fear. They learn that repair is possible, relationships can be restored, and the classroom remains a safe place to learn and belong. Over time, these small, steady choices shape a community where accountability feels human, and every student knows there is always a way forward.

Chapter 6

The Discipline Question
(What Teachers Always Wonder)

Discipline is one of the most emotionally charged parts of school life. Every adult brings their own history, beliefs, and instincts to it. Some want structure. Some want fairness. Some want calm. Some want control. Most want all of the above. But underneath every approach is the same essential question:

What are we actually trying to accomplish when a student causes harm?

This chapter helps adults pause long enough to answer that question with intention instead of habit.

What Discipline Is

Healthy discipline is:

- teaching

- boundary setting

- accountability

- repair

- relationship protection

- skill building

When adults shift from "How do I stop this?" to "What does this student need to learn?", everything changes. The tone changes. The outcome changes. The relationship changes.

What Discipline Is Not

Discipline is not:

- punishment

- revenge

- a performance for other adults

- a way to "make an example"

- a shortcut to compliance

These approaches may stop a behavior in the moment, but they don't teach anything meaningful. They don't build trust. And they don't create safer classrooms.

When adults shift from "How do I stop this?" to "What does this student need to learn?", everything changes. The tone shifts from control to curiosity.

The Three Questions Every Adult Should Ask Themselves

Before responding to harm, adults can ground themselves with three quick internal questions:

What is the actual harm? Not the annoyance. Not the inconvenience. The harm.

What does this student need to learn? A skill? A boundary? A repair strategy? A regulation tool?

What response will teach that? This keeps the adult aligned with purpose instead of emotion.

19

These three questions prevent overreactions, underreactions, and reactive discipline that escalates instead of heals.

⭐ When Restorative Practice Isn't the Only Support a Child Needs

Restorative Practice should always be part of how we respond to harm, but it isn't always the only support a child needs.

Some students have trauma histories, chemical or neurological differences, or developmental challenges that-make certain restorative steps difficult or temporarily inaccessible. These students may require additional plans, supports, or interventions tailored to their needs.

When severe harm has occurred, firm and consistent boundaries are necessary to protect the safety of others. A student may need restricted access to certain peers or spaces until repair can happen. And for some children with significant physical, neurological, or emotional challenges, full repair may not be possible in the traditional sense. In those cases, behavioral, emotional, or physical support services through the district become essential.

But no matter how firm the boundaries are, one thing never changes: The child is treated with dignity and respect. Firm does not mean punitive. Safety does not require shame. Boundaries can be clear without being cruel.

⭐ *The Question That Changes the Tone*

There is one question it took me an embarrassingly long time to understand the power of: *"What do you need?"*

20

It's simple, but profound. When a child is dysregulated, defensive, or overwhelmed, adults often jump straight to correction. But asking "What do you need?" invites the child into the process. It tells them they are not a problem to be fixed — they are a human who can participate in their own repair.

Sometimes they don't know the answer. Sometimes they guess. Sometimes they surprise you. But the question itself communicates safety, dignity, and partnership.

Adding the Administrator Layer

And this question isn't just for children. It's something administrators need to remember when they are working with staff. Adults also shut down, get overwhelmed, or feel unheard.

Asking a teacher, "What do you need?" communicates the same dignity and partnership we offer students. It shifts the conversation from evaluation to support, from pressure to collaboration.

Sometimes the teacher needs clarity. Sometimes they need time. Sometimes they need someone to listen. And sometimes they don't know what they need until someone asks. The question itself creates safety — and safe adults create safe classrooms.

For adults, it opens a door to honesty and support. When leaders ask it of staff, and staff ask it of students, the entire culture shifts toward connection instead of control. This question — "What do you need?" — changes everything. For students, it opens a door to regulation and repair.

And because not every child arrives with the same capacity for regulation or repair, the next chapter turns toward the students who need us to understand them most deeply.

Chapter 7

Students with Trauma or Chemical/ Neurological Challenges

Not every child arrives at school with the same nervous system capacity. Some come carrying trauma. Some come wired differently. Some come with both. And none of it is their fault.

Teachers see the impact long before anyone names it. It shows up in the small moments — the transitions, the group work, the unexpected changes, the social bumps — where a child's nervous system reveals what it can and cannot manage yet.

These children are not trying to make school harder. They are trying to survive their own internal experience.

What Trauma and Neurological Differences Look Like in a Classroom

Not clinical. Not diagnostic. Just the lived reality teachers face every day:

quick escalation

shutdown

avoidance

perfectionism

impulsivity

sensory overwhelm

"defiance" that is actually fear

"disrespect" that is actually dysregulation

These behaviors are not personality traits. They are nervous system responses.

What Teachers Feel

Even the most skilled educators feel:

frustration

confusion

helplessness

fear of "doing it wrong"

exhaustion

These feelings are not signs of failure. They are signs that the work is heavy and human.

The Nervous System Lens

When a child has experienced trauma or has a neurological difference, their nervous system is working harder than it looks. What seems like misbehavior is often a survival response. Their brain is scanning for threat, even in safe places. Their body reacts before their thinking brain can catch up.

This is not a choice. This is not disrespect. This is biology.

A dysregulated nervous system cannot access skills it doesn't have yet. It cannot reflect, reason, or repair until it feels safe enough to do so. And safety is not the same as calm. Safety is the sense that the adult in front of them is steady, predictable, and not going to shame them for struggling.

This is why some children cannot jump straight into restorative conversations. It is not that they won't. It's that they can't yet.

⭐ *Why Early Childhood Is Especially Challenging*

Pre-K and kindergarten are often the hardest places to practice restorative work.

Not because the children are "bad," but because their nervous systems are still under construction.

Some have never been in a structured group before. Some come from homes with inconsistent boundaries, shifting caregivers, or chronic stress. Some come from homes filled with love but lacking predictability. Some simply have developing brains that need more time.

Their behavior is communication. Their communication is often nonverbal. And their communication is often misunderstood.

⭐ *Why Some Children Cannot Reflect Yet*

Reflection requires:

language

self-awareness

emotional regulation

a sense of safety

access to the thinking brain

25

Many young learners — especially those living with trauma or chronic dysregulation — do not have consistent access to these capacities.

When a child shrugs, says "I don't know," or melts down even more, it isn't defiance. It's development. It's biology. It's the simple truth that they cannot name a need they have never felt safe enough to explore.

This does not mean they won't ever reflect. It means they cannot reflect yet.

The Heart of the Work

Understanding the nervous system changes everything. The behavior stops feeling personal. The child stops looking oppositional. The adult stops feeling like they're failing.

This chapter is the lens. It explains the "why" behind what teachers see. It lays the foundation for the work that comes next.

And the work that comes next — the how — begins in Chapter 8.

Chapter 8

What These Children Need From Us

Children with trauma histories, neurological differences, or under-developed nervous systems are not trying to make our work harder. They are trying to survive their own internal experience. What they need from adults is not perfection — it's steadiness.

Some children cannot yet name what they feel or what they need. Some cannot reflect in the moment. Some cannot repair right away. This is not defiance. It is development. Our role is to meet them where they are and guide them toward where they can grow.

What These Children Need From the Adults Around Them

1. Adults who stay regulated even when the room is not

A child's nervous system borrows the adult's. When we are steady, they have a chance to steady.

When we escalate, they escalate faster. Our calm is not softness — it is leadership.

2. Predictable routines and predictable responses

Predictability is safety. Safety is what allows the thinking brain to come back online. When children know what will happen next — and how adults will respond — their bodies can settle.

3. Boundaries delivered with dignity

Boundaries are not punishments. They are anchors. Clear, steady limits help children feel held, not controlled. A boundary delivered with frustration feels like rejection. A boundary delivered with steadiness feels like safety.

4. Separation of the child from the behavior

The behavior is communication. The child is still worthy of connection. When adults hold this distinction, shame loses its power.

5. Simplicity in the moment Fewer words. Fewer directions. Less movement. Simplicity helps the child's body settle and makes the next step possible.

6. Connection paired with structure

"Here's the limit, and I'm staying with you while you navigate it." This is the heart of restorative practice with young learners.

7. Time

Regulation is not instant. Repair is not instant. Skill-building is not instant. Children grow in uneven, unpredictable steps — and that is normal.

8. Collaboration among adults

No one adult can hold all of this alone. When adults communicate and stay aligned, the child experiences predictability — which is regulation.

Holding the Space

When a young child is dysregulated, the most important variable in the room is not the script, the strategy, or the sequence — it's the adult nervous system.

Holding the space means:

staying steady when the child cannot

communicating safety through tone and posture

reducing stimulation instead of increasing it

protecting the relationship while holding the boundary

allowing time for the child to return to themselves

staying aligned with colleagues so the child experiences

Holding the space is not about fixing the moment. It's about containing it with dignity so the child can come back into themselves. This is the groundwork that makes repair possible.

Developmentally Appropriate Repair

Repair with young children is simple, brief, and supported. It is not a test of maturity. It is a practice — one small step at a time.

Examples include:

handing back a marker

offering a picture or gesture of kindness

rebuilding one block of a knocked-down tower

helping restore the environment after a disruption

29

These moments are wonderful — but they are not the expectation. They are opportunities, not indicators of where a child 'should' be.

The aim is not to push every child toward deeper reflection. Although deeper reflection is our ultimate goal, the focus is to meet each child's nervous system where it is and support the next small step forward.

The Thread Through All of This

predictable structure

simple narrative

one small step

no shame

adult-guided

matched to the child's nervous system

Young children do not need perfect adults. They need adults who stay steady within themselves, who see the need beneath the behavior, and who respond with dignity.

This is the quiet, heartfelt, hard, and deeply caring work that changes lives. This is where repair begins — and where the foundations for everything that follows are built.

Chapter 9

The Adult Work

Children learn repair by watching us. They learn safety from how we speak to each other, how we hold boundaries, and how we return to relationship after rupture. The adult work is not extra — it is the model children inherit.

Modeling Vulnerability

Children don't need perfect adults. They need honest ones. When adults name mistakes, acknowledge impact, and show value for a relationship, children learn that being human is not something to hide.

Vulnerability in schools is simple and steady:

"I missed that."

"I spoke too quickly."

"I want to repair something between us."

"I can do better next time."

Not dramatic. Not self-punishing. Not a confession booth. Just grounded truth. When adults model this kind of vulnerability with students and each other, children learn:

mistakes are survivable

honesty is safe

repair is normal

relationships can hold discomfort

This is the kind of vulnerability that builds trust — not by being emotional, but by being real. And this matters across the many teams teachers and leaders are part of. Grade-level teams, PLCs, IEP teams, leadership teams, intervention teams — all of them depend on adults being able to say, "I don't know yet," "I need help," or "Show me how you do that." Vulnerability is what keeps collaboration honest and instructional practice growing.

And we can't forget a sense of humor. Teams thrive when adults can laugh at themselves, release tension, and remember they're human. Humor keeps vulnerability from feeling heavy — it turns learning into something shared instead of something judged.

And don't forget the chocolate.

When adults model this kind of vulnerability — with each other and with students — children learn that mistakes are survivable, honesty is safe, and repair is normal.

⭐ Modeling Accountability

Accountability is not punishment. It's clarity. Children learn responsibility when adults show them what it looks like to own impact without shame, defensiveness, or blame.

In schools, accountability sounds like:

"I see how that affected you."

"I should have checked in sooner."

"Let's reset and move forward."

"Here's what I'll do differently next time."

Short. Steady. No drama.

Accountability is not about fault — it's about repair. It's the adult version of what we want children to practice:

noticing impact

taking responsibility

making a plan

returning to relationship

When adults model this with each other, children learn that accountability is not something to fear — it's something that strengthens trust.

⭐ *Adult-to-Adult Repair*

Children watch how adults repair. They notice tone, timing, body language, and whether adults return to each other with dignity or distance.

When adults avoid repair, children learn avoidance. When adults repair with steadiness, children learn courage.

Repair between adults doesn't need to be long or emotional. It just needs to be real.

It sounds like:

"I want to repair something between us."

"My tone was sharp earlier. I'm sorry."

"I misunderstood you. Can we reset?"

"I care about our working relationship."

And this matters with students too.

When adults are willing to apologize to children — simply, sincerely, without over-explaining — kids learn that power doesn't excuse harm and that repair is something everyone practices. A quiet "I'm sorry I rushed you" or "I didn't listen as well as I should have" teaches more about dignity than any lesson plan.

Repair is not about blame — it's about restoring connection so the work can move forward with trust. When adults practice this with each other and with students, children learn that relationships can bend without breaking.

This is the kind of repair that builds a school where people feel safe to be human.

Leadership's Emotional Tone

A school can't be more regulated than its leadership. Children and staff borrow the nervous system of the adults who set the tone. When leaders move with steadiness, clarity, and repair, the whole building breathes easier.

Leadership tone isn't about being calm all the time — it's about being consistent, approachable, and willing to repair when needed.

It sounds like:

"Let's slow down and look at this together."

"I hear you."

"We can fix this."

"I want us to stay connected through this."

When leaders model emotional regulation, staff feel safer to be human. When leaders model repair, staff feel safer to take risks. When leaders model boundaries, staff feel safer to set their own.

Leadership tone becomes the emotional climate of the school — and children feel it long before they can name it.

Closing — Chapter 9

The adult work is the model children inherit. Every moment of honesty, repair, collaboration, humor, and steadiness becomes part of the emotional blueprint they carry forward. When adults practice these skills with each other — consistently, quietly, and without perfection — schools become places where everyone feels safe enough to learn, grow, and return to relationship.

This is how a restorative culture is built: one steady adult moment at a time.

Chapter 10

Why This Matters for School Culture

School culture is shaped by how adults treat each other. When honesty, repair, collaboration, and humor are part of daily practice, the building becomes a place where people feel safe to learn, try, and grow.

Children feel it. Staff feel it. Families feel it.

A culture built on steady adult relationships creates:

clearer communication

calmer classrooms

stronger teams

And it creates a school children actually want to come to. When the emotional climate is predictable and warm, attendance improves. Kids have fewer stomachaches, fewer "I don't feel good" moments, and fewer trips to the nurse.

Their bodies stop signaling danger, and they can settle into learning.

It's also a draw for parents.

Family involvement and presence is crucial for a complete school community. Many families — especially those who've felt intimidated or out of place in school settings — relax when they enter a building where adults treat each other with respect and steadiness.

When the culture is welcoming and relational, parents feel safe, valued, and included. And when they learn this approach alongside the school, it strengthens not just their confidence, but their whole family's well-being.

This isn't extra work — it is the work.

The emotional tone adults set becomes the climate students learn in.

Chapter 11

Implementation: How to Start
(and Sustain) RP

Restorative practices begin with the adults. Before teachers can lead circles with students, they need to experience what trust, safety, and community feel like for themselves. Staff training is not an add-on; it is the foundation.

When adults learn together in circles, they begin to understand the emotional rhythm, the pacing, and the vulnerability that make this work meaningful. Restorative practice should live inside staff gatherings — through shared circles, conversation, and practice. A deeper dive into this book, along with additional trainings, can strengthen understanding and help staff embody the work more fully.

Teachers need to see and feel a trusting circle. They need to know that everyone—leaders included—is learning and growing, just like the students. Mistakes are expected. No one is supposed to be perfect. What matters is authenticity and willingness. Providing teachers with prompts, language guides, and opportunities to ask for help removes the pressure to "get it right" and replaces it with shared responsibility.

Time is always a concern in schools, and teachers often worry that circles will take away from instruction. They need reassurance that building trust early saves time later — and that instruction can happen in circles, which only deepens connection. Some students may act out at first because they feel uncomfortable or aren't yet able to regulate. Calm redirection is appropriate, and if a student needs to step aside temporarily, the rest of the class will understand that the teacher is protecting the group. Over time, students may even want to address the behavior themselves and express how it affected them. This is part of the community learning process.

Good staff training is clear, simple, and supported. When possible, information can be presented in a circle with pair shares and group reflection. When time is short, PowerPoint slides, handouts, and video examples work well. What matters most is that training feels doable and powerful. Teachers need to feel the connection circles create and the difference they make. This often happens quickly—sometimes after just one meeting. Sharing success stories from real classrooms also builds confidence and buy-in.

Modeling is essential.

Staff meeting circles are a natural place to demonstrate tone, pacing, and vulnerability. But teachers also need to see how a classroom circle works when addressing an issue. Playacting a class scenario during a staff meeting can be incredibly helpful. Leaders can also offer to co-lead or observe circles in classrooms so teachers feel supported rather than alone.

Resources such as Circle Forward: Building a Restorative School Community (Boyes-Watson & Pranis, 2015) provide practical guidance and scenarios that teachers can use immediately.

39

Structure matters.

Teachers should model and teach the three core agreements: Speak from the heart. Listen with your heart. Say just enough. A talking piece—chosen or created by the class—helps maintain order, signals that this is a special moment and gives each student a clear moment to speak or pass. Students who struggle to sit still can be offered fidgets to help regulate their bodies so they can stay present in the circle.

The non-negotiables of staff training are simple: consistency, check-ins, kind accountability, and ongoing practice. Teachers must know that support is available—through the principal, dean, counselor, or any trained staff member—whenever they feel unsure.

Leaders play a crucial role. They must be authentic, willing to learn alongside their staff, and committed to emphasizing the benefits of restorative practices. Their tone sets the tone. When leaders offer clarity, support, and honest answers (or a willingness to find them), teachers feel safe enough to try. Ultimately, staff training matters because significance and belonging matter. Everyone learns best when they feel safe and valued.

Restorative practices are not a strategy to implement; they are a culture to build. And that culture begins with the adults.

Morning Circles

Morning circles are a simple, predictable way to begin the day with connection. Students sit where they can see one another, share briefly, and listen to the stories and experiences that shape their classmates. This daily check-in builds significance and belonging, and it gives teachers a quick read on how students are arriving emotionally.

If a child has something personal to share that requires privacy, the teacher can follow up individually or involve support staff.

Over time, the trust built in these circles creates a safe environment where students take risks, speak honestly, and receive correction without feeling diminished. Morning circles set the emotional tone for the day and lay the groundwork for deeper restorative work when it's needed.

Classroom Instruction in Circles

Instruction can also take place in a circle, and doing so strengthens the sense of community. Many lessons—math discussions, science conversations, story-writing ideas, problem-solving, and social-emotional learning—work beautifully in this format. The circle invites students to think together, listen to one another, and build shared understanding. Desks can be used later for practice work, but the circle is where ideas are explored and voices are heard.

Simple hand-raising works to maintain order and gives each student a chance to make mistakes and learn. Students who struggle to sit still can use fidgets to help regulate their bodies.

When instruction happens in a circle, it reinforces trust, belonging, and the belief that every voice matters.

41

For students, circles become a place where they feel seen, heard, and valued. Over time, they learn that their voice matters and that the voices of others matter too. The predictability of circles—whether in the morning or during moments of repair—creates a sense of safety that many children have never experienced in a group setting. Students begin to relax into the rhythm of listening, sharing, and being part of something larger than themselves. Even the most hesitant or active students find their place, whether through the option to pass, the support of a fidget, or the steady presence of a caring adult.

As trust grows, students take more risks, show more empathy, and learn to address issues respectfully. Circles help them understand that community is something they build together, one conversation at a time, and that they matter.

Chapter 12

Roles: Teachers, Recess Coaches, Counselors, Leadership

Restorative practices work best when everyone in the school community shares a common language. When adults use the same words, expectations, and approaches, students feel safer and more confident because the emotional rules don't change from room to room. Each role in the building contributes to this shared language in its own way. No one carries restorative practices alone; instead, the whole community works together to create a predictable, supportive environment where every child feels seen, valued, and connected. The following descriptions highlight how each role helps build and sustain that culture.

Principal

The principal sets the tone for restorative practices in the building. Their role is to model authenticity, support staff as learners, and reinforce the belief that

every child deserves to feel significant and that they belong.

It helps when principals visit classroom circles occasionally and participate in staff circles themselves. When challenges arise, they respond with curiosity and support rather than judgment, helping maintain a culture of trust.

Principals also support teachers by helping them find the time, tools, and encouragement they need so students and staff can move forward safely and respectfully.

Dean or Behavior Specialist

The dean supports teachers in addressing behavior through restorative approaches rather than punitive ones. They help facilitate repair circles, coach teachers through difficult situations, and step in when a classroom issue needs additional guidance. Their role is to help students understand the impact of their actions and to support teachers in maintaining a safe, connected learning environment.

When a situation goes beyond what RP can address, the dean works with the principal and counselor to bring in additional resources, interventions, or supports for the student.

The dean is also often the point person for restorative practices in the building, ensuring that new staff are brought up to speed and that ongoing training stays consistent.

School Counselor

The counselor brings emotional insight and developmental understanding to the restorative process. They help students prepare for repair conversations, support those who need extra time or privacy, and collaborate with teachers to understand underlying needs. Counselors often co-facilitate circles, especially when emotions run high, and they help ensure that every child feels seen and supported.

Classroom Teacher

Teachers are the daily builders of community. They lead morning circles, use instructional circles to strengthen connection, and guide students through small moments of repair.

Their role is to create a classroom where students feel safe, valued, and responsible to one another. Teachers model calm, consistency, and curiosity, helping students learn how to listen, speak honestly, and solve problems together.

Support Staff (Paraeducators, Specialists, Office Staff)

Support staff help carry the culture throughout the building. They greet students, reinforce expectations with kindness, and participate in circles when appropriate.

Their steady presence helps students feel known beyond the classroom.

On the playground, support staff play a key role in noticing small conflicts early, guiding students through quick restorative conversations, and helping them return to play with repaired relationships.

These short, simple interactions prevent bigger issues and reinforce the idea that community exists everywhere, not just in the classroom.

Student Recess Coaches

Some fifth- and sixth-grade students—depending on the size and structure of the elementary school—can be trained as recess coaches to support younger students on the playground. These students are carefully selected: they must be interested, responsible, and ready for the role. Once trained, they use simple tion strategies to help guide peers through small disagreements and quick repair conversations

Once trained, they use simple facilitation strategies to help guide peers through small disagreements and quick repair conversations.

Recess coaches model empathy, responsibility, and calm problem-solving, and the role deepens their own understanding of restorative practices. It gives them a meaningful sense of significance and belonging, as well as a leadership opportunity as they contribute to the well-being of the school community.

Students

Students are active participants in building their community. They learn to listen, share, take responsibility, and repair harm when needed. Their role is to show up as themselves, practice empathy, and contribute to a classroom where everyone feels safe and valued. Over time, students become leaders in the process, reminding one another of norms and helping maintain the trust they've built together.

Closing

When everyone in the building plays their part, restorative practices become more than a strategy — they become a culture. The next chapter explores how we keep that culture strong in the long view.

Chapter 13

The Long View: Why I Focus on Elementary Schools

I focus on elementary schools for a reason. This is where the foundation is built. By the time students reach middle and high school, their patterns of regulation, belonging, communication, and repair are already taking shape. Secondary educators can absolutely use restorative practices — and many do, beautifully — but they are often working to re-teach what was never taught early enough.

Elementary schools are different. They are the first community children experience outside of their families. They are where students learn how to name feelings, navigate conflict, trust adults, trust themselves, and repair harm. These are not "extras." They are the emotional and relational skills that make learning possible.

Elementary school is also where children's nervous systems learn what safety feels like in a group — a foundation that shapes every future learning environment.

When we build this foundation early, students carry it forward. Middle and high schools don't have to start from scratch. They get students who already know how to regulate, reflect, reconnect, and repair. They can build on it instead of scrambling to teach it in crisis. And when these skills are taught early, we give every child — not just the naturally regulated or socially confident ones — a fair chance to thrive.

Closing Reflection

At the center of everything we do in schools is relationship. The small moments of connection — the shared laugh, the gentle check-in, the quiet "I see you" — are what make learning and growth possible. Throughout my career, those moments were the heartbeat of my work. They helped students return to themselves, reminded them they mattered, and built the trust that made growth possible.

Restorative practices simply give shape to what educators have always known: children thrive when they feel safe, valued, and connected. When we lead with relationship, we create the conditions where regulation, repair, and resilience can take root. My hope is that this book encourages you to keep those human moments at the center of your practice. They are where the real transformation begins.

Restorative Practices cannot thrive on enthusiasm alone.

They require leadership that is willing to model vulnerability, consistency, and relational courage. Some leaders will embrace this immediately. Others will need support, reassurance, and time. But the ones who fear vulnerability the most are often the ones most changed by it. When leaders commit to this work — truly commit — schools transform. Not because of a program, but because of a culture.

When adults feel heard, safety grows.

When adults feel valued, trust deepens.

Restorative Practices thrive in communities built on connection.

48

Sally Emiline "The End" Page

From the Sally Emiline children's series

The End... and also the beginning.

If Sally Emiline were here, she'd probably give a little shrug, a half-smile, and say something like, "Well... we did it." And she'd be right. Because every ending in this work is really just another beginning — another chance to connect, to listen, to repair, to try again.

Schools are full of imperfect, beautiful, human moments. And that's the good news. Because it means we get to show up as humans too — with warmth, humor, patience, and the belief that every child can grow.

So here's to the next circle, the next conversation, the next small moment that makes a big difference. Here's to the work that continues long after the last page is turned.

The end. And the beginning.

QUESTIONS FOR REFLECTION

Seeing Children Clearly

- What shifts when I view a child's behavior through the lens of unmet needs rather than misbehavior?

- How does my own nervous system influence the way I respond to students?

- Where in my practice do I default to control instead of connection?

- What patterns do I notice in the children who challenge me the most?

- How might I create more predictability, clarity, and emotional safety in my classroom or school?

- What does "repair" look like in my daily interactions with students?

Seeing Ourselves Clearly

- When a child is dysregulated, what story do I tell myself about what's happening?

- How do I signal to students that they are safe with me, even when things go wrong?

- Which adult responses in my school strengthen relationships, and which unintentionally strain them?

- How do I model emotional regulation for the children watching me?

- What small, consistent actions could build trust over time?

• Which restorative practices are already working well in our school, and why?

• Where do we see gaps between our intentions and our daily routines?

• How do we support staff who are overwhelmed or unsure how to respond to student behavior?

• What systems or structures could we adjust to reduce escalation and increase connection?

• What is one change we can implement this month that would improve emotional safety for students?

Core References

Boyes-Watson, C., & Pranis, K. (2015). Circle Forward: Building a Restorative School Community. Living Justice Press.

International Institute for Restorative Practices (IIRP). Restorative Practices Handbook for Teachers, Disciplinarians, and Administrators.

Dreikurs, R. Selected works on belonging, significance, and Adlerian approaches to behavior.

Circle practices used by First Nations communities such as Hollow Water, Carcross-Tagish, and Dahka T'lingit.

Peacemaking traditions of the Navajo Nation.

Māori family group conferencing, which influenced modern youth justice systems.

Additional Recommended Reading

Smith, D., Fisher, D., & Frey, N. Better Than Carrots or Sticks: Restorative Practices for Positive Classroom Management.

Amstutz, L. S., & Mullet, J. H. The Little Book of Restorative Discipline for Schools.

Greene, R. Lost at School: Why Our Kids with Behavioral Challenges Are Falling Through the Cracks and How We Can Help Them.

Barter, D., et al. The Restorative Practices Playbook (various editions).

Children's Books by Renee That Support Emotional Literacy and Restorative Practices:

These titles introduce emotional regulation, belonging, and relational repair in ways that are accessible to young children. They pair naturally with the practices described in this book and can be used in classrooms, small groups, or family settings.

Kenady, R. Sally Emiline series:

Seriously, No Way

Dealing With Mad Isn't Easy

Holy Moly

Next to come: Cuckoo Clock -

Understanding children who are full of energy for a variety of reasons and discovering tools that can help.

Credits

Created by Martha Renee Creative
A registered DBA of Kenady Enterprises /
Visit: KenadyCollections.com

Inspired by my career experiences in
education, youth services
and life in general.

With deep gratitude, this book is dedicated to the children,
families and educators whose patience, understanding and
wholehearted dedication light the way.
To those who have challenged their own vulnerability
and accountability to bring Restorative Practices to life-
Your hard work, and the giving of your heart and soul,
has supported children into becoming their best selves.

This journey was a gift: a shared commitment to giving
every voice a place to be heard.
Also, thanks to my digital collaborator, Microsoft Copi-
lot, for helping me shape ideas, smooth the words, and
bring "Perspective" to life.